Francis Frith's
AROUND HORSHAM

◆

PHOTOGRAPHIC MEMORIES

Francis Frith's
AROUND HORSHAM

◆

Martin Andrew

FRITH
BOOK Co

First published in the United Kingdom in 2000 by
Frith Book Company Ltd

Hardback Edition 2000
ISBN 1-85937-127-2

Paperback Edition 2001
ISBN 1-85937-432-8

Reprinted in Hardback 2001

British Library Cataloguing in Publication Data

Francis Frith's Around Horsham
Martin Andrew

Frith Book Company Ltd
Frith's Barn, Teffont,
Salisbury, Wiltshire SP3 5QP
Tel: +44 (0) 1722 716 376
Email: info@frithbook.co.uk
www.frithbook.co.uk

Printed and bound in Great Britain

AS WITH ANY HISTORICAL DATABASE THE FRITH ARCHIVE IS CONSTANTLY BEING CORRECTED AND IMPROVED
AND THE PUBLISHERS WOULD WELCOME INFORMATION ON OMISSIONS OR INACCURACIES

CONTENTS

Francis Frith: Victorian Pioneer   7

Frith's Archive - A Unique Legacy   10

Around Horsham - An Introduction   12

From the South: The Parish Church,

The Causeway and The Town Hall   18

The Carfax   33

Horsham Town Centre   45

Horsham Park & Some Other Buildings   59

Around Horsham   65

Index   83

Free Mounted Print Voucher   87

FRANCIS FRITH: *Victorian Pioneer*

FRANCIS FRITH, Victorian founder of the world-famous photographic archive, was a complex and multitudinous man. A devout Quaker and a highly successful Victorian businessman, he was both philosophic by nature and pioneering in outlook.

By 1855 Francis Frith had already established a wholesale grocery business in Liverpool, and sold it for the astonishing sum of £200,000, which is the equivalent today of over £15,000,000. Now a multi-millionaire, he was able to indulge his passion for travel. As a child he had pored over travel books written by early explorers, and his fancy and imagination had been stirred by family holidays to the sublime mountain regions of Wales and Scotland. 'What a land of spirit-stirring and enriching scenes and places!' he had written. He was to return to these scenes of grandeur in later years to 'recapture the thousands of vivid and tender memories', but with a different purpose. Now in his thirties, and captivated by the new science of photography, Frith set out on a series of pioneering journeys to the Nile regions that occupied him from 1856 until 1860.

INTRIGUE AND ADVENTURE

He took with him on his travels a specially-designed wicker carriage that acted as both dark-room and sleeping chamber. These far-flung journeys were packed with intrigue and adventure. In his life story, written when he was sixty-three, Frith tells of being held captive by bandits, and of fighting 'an awful midnight battle to the very point of surrender with a deadly pack of hungry, wild dogs'. Sporting flowing Arab costume, Frith arrived at Akaba by camel seventy years before Lawrence, where he encountered 'desert princes and rival sheikhs, blazing with jewel-hilted swords'.

During these extraordinary adventures he was assiduously exploring the desert regions bordering the Nile and patiently recording the antiquities and peoples with his camera. He was the first photographer to venture beyond the sixth cataract. Africa was still the mysterious 'Dark Continent', and Stanley and Livingstone's historic meeting was a decade into the future. The conditions for picture taking confound belief. He laboured for hours in his wicker dark-room in the sweltering heat of the desert, while the volatile chemicals fizzed dangerously in their trays. Often he was forced to work in remote tombs and caves where conditions were cooler. Back in London he exhibited his photographs and was 'rapturously cheered' by members of the Royal Society. His reputation as a photographer was made overnight. An eminent modern historian has likened their impact on the population of the time to that on our own generation of the first photographs taken on the surface of the moon.

VENTURE OF A LIFE-TIME

Characteristically, Frith quickly spotted the opportunity to create a new business as a specialist publisher of photographs. He lived in an era of immense and sometimes violent change. For the poor in the early part of Victoria's reign work was a drudge and the hours long, and people had precious little free time to enjoy themselves.

Most had no transport other than a cart or gig at their disposal, and had not travelled far beyond the boundaries of their own town or village. However, by the 1870s, the railways had threaded their way across the country, and Bank Holidays and half-day Saturdays had been made obligatory by Act of Parliament. All of a sudden the ordinary working man and his family were able to enjoy days out and see a little more of the world.

With characteristic business acumen, Francis Frith foresaw that these new tourists would enjoy having souvenirs to commemorate their days out. In 1860 he married Mary Ann Rosling and set out with the intention of photographing every city, town and village in Britain. For the next thirty years he travelled the country by train and by pony and trap, producing fine photographs of seaside resorts and beauty spots that were keenly bought by millions of Victorians. These prints were painstakingly pasted into family albums and pored over during the dark nights of winter, rekindling precious memories of summer excursions.

THE RISE OF FRITH & CO

Frith's studio was soon supplying retail shops all over the country. To meet the demand he gathered about him a small team of photographers, and published the work of independent artist-photographers of the calibre of Roger Fenton and Francis Bedford. In order to gain some understanding of the scale of Frith's business one only has to look at the catalogue issued by Frith & Co in 1886: it runs to some 670

pages, listing not only many thousands of views of the British Isles but also many photographs of most European countries, and China, Japan, the USA and Canada – note the sample page shown above from the hand-written *Frith & Co* ledgers detailing pictures taken. By 1890 Frith had created the greatest specialist photographic publishing company in the world, with over 2,000 outlets – more than the combined number that Boots and WH Smith have today! The picture on the right shows the *Frith & Co* display board at Ingleton in the Yorkshire Dales. Beautifully constructed with mahogany frame and gilt inserts, it could display up to a dozen local scenes.

POSTCARD BONANZA

The ever-popular holiday postcard we know today took many years to develop. In 1870 the Post Office issued the first plain cards, with a pre-printed stamp on one face. In 1894 they allowed other publishers' cards to be sent through the mail with an attached adhesive halfpenny stamp. Demand grew rapidly, and in 1895 a new size of postcard was permitted called the

court card, but there was little room for illustration. In 1899, a year after Frith's death, a new card measuring 5.5 x 3.5 inches became the standard format, but it was not until 1902 that the divided back came into being, with address and message on one face and a full-size illustration on the other. *Frith & Co* were in the vanguard of postcard development, and Frith's sons Eustace and Cyril continued their father's monumental task, expanding the number of views offered to the public and recording more and more places in Britain, as the coasts and countryside were opened up to mass travel.

Francis Frith died in 1898 at his villa in Cannes, his great project still growing. The archive he created continued in business for another seventy years. By 1970 it contained over a third of a million pictures of 7,000 cities, towns and villages. The massive photographic record Frith has left to us stands as a living monument to a special and very remarkable man.

Frith's Archive: *A Unique Legacy*

FRANCIS FRITH'S legacy to us today is of immense significance and value, for the magnificent archive of evocative photographs he created provides a unique record of change in 7,000 cities, towns and villages throughout Britain over a century and more. Frith and his fellow studio photographers revisited locations many times down the years to update their views, compiling for us an enthralling and colourful pageant of British life and character.

We tend to think of Frith's sepia views of Britain as nostalgic, for most of us use them to conjure up memories of places in our own lives with which we have family associations. It often makes us forget that to Francis Frith they were records of daily life as it was actually being lived in the cities, towns and villages of his day. The Victorian age was one of great and often bewildering change for ordinary people, and though the pictures evoke an impression of slower times, life was as busy and hectic as it is today.

We are fortunate that Frith was a photographer of the people, dedicated to recording the minutiae of everyday life. For it is this sheer wealth of visual data, the painstaking chronicle of changes in dress, transport, street layouts, buildings, housing, engineering and landscape that captivates us so much today. His remarkable images offer us a powerful link with the past and with the lives of our ancestors.

TODAY'S TECHNOLOGY

Computers have now made it possible for Frith's many thousands of images to be accessed almost instantly. In the Frith archive today, each photograph is carefully 'digitised' then stored on a CD Rom. Frith archivists can locate a single photograph amongst thousands within seconds. Views can be catalogued and sorted under a variety of categories of place and content to the immediate benefit of researchers. Inexpensive reference prints can be created for them at the touch of a mouse button, and a wide range of books and other printed materials assembled and published for a wider, more general readership - in the next twelve months over a hundred Frith local history titles will be published! The

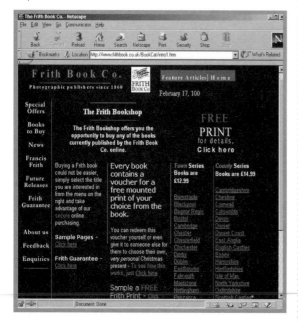

See Frith at www. frithbook.co.uk

day-to-day workings of the archive are very different from how they were in Francis Frith's time: imagine the herculean task of sorting through eleven tons of glass negatives as Frith had to do to locate a particular sequence of pictures! Yet the archive still prides itself on maintaining the same high standards of excellence laid down by Francis Frith, including the painstaking cataloguing and indexing of every view.

It is curious to reflect on how the internet now allows researchers in America and elsewhere greater instant access to the archive than Frith himself ever enjoyed. Many thousands of individual views can be called up on screen within seconds on one of the Frith internet sites, enabling people living continents away to revisit the streets of their ancestral home town, or view places in Britain where they have enjoyed holidays. Many overseas researchers welcome the chance to view special theme selections, such as transport, sports, costume and ancient monuments.

We are certain that Francis Frith would have heartily approved of these modern developments, for he himself was always working at the very limits of Victorian photographic technology.

THE VALUE OF THE ARCHIVE TODAY

Because of the benefits brought by the computer, Frith's images are increasingly studied by social historians, by researchers into genealogy and ancestory, by architects, town planners, and by teachers and schoolchildren involved in local history projects. In addition, the archive offers every one of us a unique opportunity to examine the places where we and our families have lived and worked down the years. Immensely successful in Frith's own era, the archive is now, a century and more on, entering a new phase of popularity.

THE PAST IN TUNE WITH THE FUTURE

Historians consider the Francis Frith Collection to be of prime national importance. It is the only archive of its kind remaining in private ownership and has been valued at a million pounds. However, this figure is now rapidly increasing as digital technology enables more and more people around the world to enjoy its benefits.

Francis Frith's archive is now housed in an historic timber barn in the beautiful village of Teffont in Wiltshire. Its founder would not recognize the archive office as it is today. In place of the many thousands of dusty boxes containing glass plate negatives and an all-pervading odour of photographic chemicals, there are now ranks of computer screens. He would be amazed to watch his images travelling round the world at unimaginable speeds through network and internet lines.

The archive's future is both bright and exciting. Francis Frith, with his unshakeable belief in making photographs available to the greatest number of people, would undoubtedly approve of what is being done today with his lifetime's work. His photographs, depicting our shared past, are now bringing pleasure and enlightenment to millions around the world a century and more after his death.

AROUND HORSHAM – *An Introduction*

FOR MANY PASSING through Horsham by car in the 1960s, 1970s and into the 1980s, their memory will be of stop-start crawling through narrow streets with right-angle bends. Horsham suffered greatly from traffic pressures until it finally got its western by-pass for the A24 London to Worthing Road and the northern by-pass on the A264 Crawley Road. The inner relief road, Albion Way, helps on the A281 Guildford to Brighton road. It may seem strange to start this introduction with a list of roads, but the removal of the choking through traffic has allowed the town centre, the historic core, to be transformed into a pleasant environment for shoppers and visitors. Admittedly the road improvements of Albion Way and Park Way, the northern inner relief road, did much damage to the town's historic fabric, but lessons have been learnt, and the visual and cultural assets of the town seem in far better shape now than they have done for many years. Horsham can no longer be described as a traffic-strangled town.

Indeed, Horsham retained numerous assets amid the carnage, most notably the direct link with the countryside beyond the parish church south of the young River Arun,

which rises in nearby St Leonard's Forest, and the wonderfully calm backwater of The Causeway, cut off from the bustle of the main town. Also Horsham Park, to the north of the centre, is an extremely valuable 'green lung' for the town. The centrepiece, which gets an entire chapter in this book, is The Carfax, the central market place and square; it has been superbly improved and repaved in the 1990s to the great benefit of pedestrians, shoppers and visitors.

Horsham is at the west end of the High Weald, which crosses the Kent border; it formed a muddy, well-nigh impassable barrier for many centuries between the North Downs and the sea. Virtually useless agriculturally, this is the heath and woodland of Ashdown Forest, Worth Forest and, nearest to Horsham, St Leonard's Forest, whose name first appeared in writing in 1213 as 'foresta Sancti Leonardi'. To the west, north and south of Horsham is the Low Weald, thick Wealden Clays with small, irregular fields cleared from woodland; here, isolated timber-framed farmsteads and small villages can be seen, with much residual woodland. Oak trees seem to predominate in both these woods and as standards in the hedgerows.

This is medieval and earlier farmland, and Horsham grew up as the market centre for a wide area of north Sussex. The forest produced timber and supported pigs, and some of it was turned into deer parks; the clay lands produced corn, barley, poultry, cattle and sheep. All this produce passed through the Carfax market, and much of the barley went until recently to the local brewers, King and Barnes. Quarrying of the local sandstone, the Horsham stone, produced both good building stone and strata that can be split to produce the heavy stone roof tiles that are so characteristic of the area. This material is found at all levels of society, from cottages and farmhouses to upper class houses such as Field Place or Horsham Park. But I am moving ahead too far and into the Middle Ages.

Horsham is four miles east of the Roman road from London to Chichester, the important town then known as Noviomagus Regnenses, the tribal capital of the Regnenses. This road acquired the Anglo-Saxon name of Stane Street, meaning 'stone' or 'paved'. Although there was a Roman staging post at Dedisham, near Slinfold, there is no evidence of a Roman settlement at Horsham. Sussex was conquered and settled early in the Anglo-Saxon period; indeed, it became a kingdom, the Kingdom of the South Saxons, 'Suthseaxe', not long after the ruthless Aella, the first king, and his warrior band landed near Selsey in 477 AD. Occupation of the Low Weald was slower than in the coastal plain, but place names like Billingshurst to the south and Itchingfield (featured in this book) indicate early settlement: the element '-ingas-' in the place names, meaning a people or tribe, is a particularly early one. Horsham, however, makes its first appearance in a land charter of 947 AD, surprisingly with the same spelling as now. Later the name went through some spelling variations before reverting to the 10th-century spelling, including Horsam in 1301 and Horsom in 1657. In Old English the name means 'horse settlement', so presumably the

GENERAL VIEW 1891 29711

area in those days was a centre for horse breeding.

One of the characteristics of the English settlement in Sussex was the way estates and territories (it is too early to talk of parishes) evolved: a version of Germanic transhumance farming was practised, whereby stock was reared in places well away from the centre of

Several of these tracks converged on Horsham, so it presumably became a market centre; for here there was an easy crossing of the River Arun, together with a convenient location at the west end of the great barrier of the High Weald.

Certainly, Horsham prospered. Although it is not mentioned in the Domesday Book of

ST MARY'S CHURCH 1907 58190

a settlement. Thus early on a network of north-south parallel tracks leading from the coastal villages led inland across the South Downs and into the interior where the animals were reared and pastured, particularly in the summer months. Thus the woodland was cleared and fenced, and enclosures were formed, the 'folds' which are so common as Sussex place name elements - Slinfold, for instance, to be seen in this book. Later, from the Middle Ages onwards, these tracks became sheep and cattle droves used by the stock travelling to the immense and all-consuming London market; this situation lasted well into the 19th century, when the railways effectively destroyed the old droving of herds.

1087, its parish church of St Mary has Norman stonework in the north-west part of the nave; here you can see a characteristic narrow round-arched window and two round arched doorways, one into the tower, whose lower part is also Norman. The town is referred to as a borough in 1235, and was granted an annual fair by Henry III in 1233; this was not a funfair, I should add, but a market fair, chiefly dealing in poultry and corn. The poultry in question were the fine four-clawed Dorking kind, which were highly regarded as a delicacy in London, and thus commanded a high premium. A later market charter granted by Queen Anne in 1705 shifted the emphasis from poultry to cattle. The borough was sufficiently important to send two burgesses, that is townsmen, to Parliament from 1295 onwards, making it one of the earliest-represented boroughs in the House of Commons. In 1617 Horsham obtained corporate borough status from James I, giving it a common seal and elected bailiffs. Horsham was sufficiently important a centre to be on the court circuit dispensing royal justice: from 1307 the Assizes and Quarter Sessions were held in the town, usually at the Market House, later known as the Town Hall. The last assizes were in 1830, after which they moved to Lewes.

It is now thought that the nucleus of the earliest town grew up at the junction of the present East Street, Park Street and Denne Road, where higher ground crosses the Arun valley, but the centre of gravity moved west when The Carfax became the central focus and the parish church was built at the end of The Causeway, originally a continuation of South Street. Further west, the track now known as Worthing Road became the main road south from the town, and the other two were comprehensively blocked off by the 17th-century emparking of Denne Park - this effectively rendered The Causeway and Denne Road dead ends. This was, in fact, of immense benefit to our modern appreciation of the town, for it stopped southward expansion over the River Arun dead and gives a wonderfully rural approach to the south of the town directly from the deepest countryside. The sloping fields between the Park and the river are popular with dog walkers and strollers, and it is always difficult to feel you are approaching a major town, for the church spire looks like that of a typical Sussex village church. Admittedly, it does not do to look too

closely, for the Royal and Sun Alliance office-blocks are all too apparent beyond. Still, you are in deep countryside until you cross the river on its iron footbridge. Beyond the church, The Causeway, with its wonderful collection of buildings, including one used for the very informative and attractive local museum, is cut off from the town centre by later market infill, including the old Town Hall. These three hundred yards are, again, in a completely different and tranquil world.

The centre of town is The Carfax, a market place laid out where a number of roads meet, not a crossroads. It seems to be a version of the Old French 'carrefourgs' or crossways. The name is first recorded in 1548 as 'Scarfax', but its origins must be earlier. It should be borne in mind, of course, that its huge original open area has been much encroached upon: the whole central area which includes the Nat West Bank is just such encroachment, whereby temporary market stalls become more permanent booths and then are replaced by timber-framed or brick buildings. This encroachment also screened The Causeway from the town infilling to the east of South Street.

This bustling trade area has now been largely pedestrianised, and traffic is restricted to the east side. The Carfax has been given back to the people; you can walk around in comfort and safety without choking on traffic fumes. It has been very well laid out, and is a credit to the town. However, there are minus points: the photographs of North Street in this book are a record of a long-gone street. It is now Royal and Sun Alliance territory, with three enormous office blocks and a foot-bridge over the inner relief road, Chart Way. Horsham is their headquarters, and architecturally speaking the town knows it. Albion Way itself cuts a swathe through the town with Horsham Park to its north, but it is difficult to graft massive offices into an old town's fabric without serious harm. These three blocks, Stane Court, St Mark's Court and Park Side, dominate views north-east out of The Carfax or south from the station. St Mark's Court should be singled out: no doubt attractive office block architecture by Sipson Gray Architects, completed in 1991, it wraps round and dwarfs the retained tower and spire of St Marks's Church, whose Victorian spire was such a landmark in the town. One wonders whether it was worth retaining the tower and spire in such a context.

At the west end of a pedestrianised West Street a spectacular water sculpture has recently been installed, consisting of a giant sphere which fills with water and then discharges six tons of it into a basin and four troughs in a crashing roar. This is the Shelley Fountain by Angela Connor, and is great fun. Beyond, however, is Albion Way. To the north of the immediate centre is Horsham Park, with a mansion of about 1720 in Christopher Wren style; it is now council offices. Its park is an asset to the town. On its fringes is the Hospital, a good Arts and Crafts-style building of 1922, and opposite is the former Collyer's Grammar School, now a much expanded sixth-form college. Relocated here in 1892, it was founded in 1532 in the town centre.

The bulk of Horsham's expansion took place from the mid 19th century to the north and east of the town, partly focussing around the railway station; the line, originally a branch from the London to Brighton line, arrived in 1848. Almost all this development, at least until the 1970s, took place on the former commons of the town, which were enclosed by Act of Parliament in 1813. These were about seven hundred and forty acres of 'waste' owned (and neglected) by one of the

THE CARFAX 1907 58192

major landowners in the area, the Duke of Norfolk, who was constrained to build the curious neo-Norman town hall in 1812 while the enclosure kerfuffle and controversy was under way. Certainly, without the enclosure Horsham could not easily have expanded in any direction, particularly with Denne Park and its fallow deer grazing contentedly cutting off all hope of southerly growth. The view of Rusper Road is in the heart of the enclosed land and the town's Victorian boom growth.

Also in this book is a brief tour of some of the surrounding villages, which are all well worth seeing; the centrepiece of the tour is undoubtedly the extraordinary translation of Christ's Hospital School from the soot of London's Newgate Street to the rolling Sussex countryside in 1902. Founded in 1552, with its pupils, poor boys and orphans originally organised in wards, its move to Sussex completed its transformation into a public school. From 1893 to 1902 a quadrangle of stupendously-scaled brick buildings with stone dressings rose above the surrounding countryside to designs by Aston Webb (who was responsible also for the present frontage block at Buckingham Palace) and Ingress Bell. The foundation stone ceremony came in the midst of all this, in 1897. The school even acquired its own railway station at which the blue-coated scholars would arrive and depart each term, although nowadays they all arrive by car, no doubt. The school became co-educational again in 1985 - it had had a girl's ward in the London school until 1784 - and then moved the girls to new buildings in Hertford, which they shared with the preparatory boys until 1902. The scale of the Christ's Hospital buildings must have completely overawed a new boy: as you can see in photograph

No 58198, people are dwarfed by the austere and towering buildings around the vast quadrangle. The austerity of the buildings owes something to the cost-conscious Charity Commissioners; before they approved Aston Webb's plans, they discarded what they regarded as superfluous ornament and expenditure. The effect was, I suspect, to make the complex even more monumentally overpowering. The views in the book show the school just after its completion, and are thus an even more interesting record.

Horsham is now a much more accessible and enjoyable town than it was when I lived at Haywards Heath in the 1970s. Although the modern Swan Walk shopping centre occupies much of the area north of West Street and west of The Carfax, and the Royal and Sun Alliance insurance company has taken the heart out of North Street, sufficient of quality remains to entice the visitor. The Causeway with its fine local history museum in a wonderful timber-framed house, the parish church overlooking the River Arun and the fields leading to Denne Park, the grounds of Horsham Park and the unexpected remnants of farmhouses and cottages such as those in the north part of North Street - all these make Horsham a place full of interest and incident. Its population has grown tenfold since 1800 when it was about three thousand; it reached 17,000 in 1951 and 30,000 in 1991, so it is natural that there should be great changes. But walking in from the Denne Park direction to the parish church and The Causeway shows that much of the best has survived the frantic 20th century's worst, and The Carfax is now a most attractively enhanced area, well worthy of Horsham's very important role in north Sussex's history.

GENERAL VIEW 1891 29711

The emparking of Denne Park in the 17th century, while
at the time closing off the main road south out of this
prosperous market town, still has its effect, for the view
of the town from the south is still remarkably unchanged
and rural. Admittedly, the backdrop has the office blocks
of Albion Way to remind us of the 20th century.

FROM DENNE PARK 1895 35040

Looking north-east from the high point of the footpath across the fields, two of the trees in the middle distance survive; beyond is the railway running across the fields between neat thorn hedges. A later footbridge crosses the railway line, and the path leads to the church, whose shingled spire was then the tallest structure in the town.

THE CRICKET GROUND 1927 79610

A later Frith photographer has shifted his camera angle to the left to view the Horsham Cricket Ground with a game in full swing. This was once known as the Barrack Field, for during the Napoleonic Wars, from 1797 to 1814, Horsham was inundated with soldiers, and this was part of their parade grounds and barrack area. The cricket club still flourishes, but with grander pavilions and clubhouse.

THE CAUSEWAY 1898 41922

This view is definitely not the well-known Causeway in the town, but is the Worthing Road of a century ago. To the right is Denne Park; in the woods on the left can be glimpsed the small tower, little more than a battlemented garden building, which until the 1920s stood near the junction of Tower Hill and the Worthing Road.

ST MARY'S CHURCH 1907 58190

Crossing the railway you come to the young River Arun, with beyond it St Mary's Church and behind that the town. The church, with its charming shingled broach spire, has a villagey feeling, rather than an urban one, and gives little clue to the large market town beyond. This view is now sadly obscured by the modern houses of Fordingbridge Close.

THE RIVER ARUN 1923 73410

MILL BAY 1927 79614

THE RIVER ARUN 1923
This view, further west along the river bank, shows the iron footbridge on the right which is on the line of the old main road out of town until it was severed in the 17th century by Denne Park. This preserved The Causeway and these fields as a backwater - to their immeasurable benefit. The ancient oaks have since gone, and this view should be compared with photographs Nos 79614 and 79613.

MILL BAY 1927
Looking west along the north bank, we see the curiously ramshackle fencing surrounding a Garden of Remembrance laid out soon after photograph No 73410 had been taken. The big trees sheltering it have long gone, and the garden has been more formalised with hedging and timber fencing. The river bank is now dense with poplars and alders with the occasional sycamore.

THE GARDEN OF REMEMBRANCE 1927 79613

Just over the footbridge, this view should be compared with No 73410. The brick bridge over the parallel stream survives, but the Garden of Remembrance occupies the area closest to the river. At this time there was a motley collection of 'rustic' seats and archways, as well as the odd salvaged iron railing sections supporting lines of hanging baskets.

THE TOWN MILL 1891 29722

As we look west towards Town Mill, the view is now much changed. The mill pond to the left is filled in, and the Arun banks are tree-lined, mostly by alders and poplars. The tall building of the old watermill survives and is now offices, retaining its old painted sign 'Provender Mill', but the cottages and other buildings to its right have all gone, to be replaced by offices and flats.

MILL BAY 1923 73409

MILL BAY 1923
Nearer Town Mill, the cottage to the right of the mill has gone, and the area has been attractively landscaped. The river path is a popular stroll for schoolchildren on their way to St Mary's School, dog walkers and lunchtime office workers. The whole area south of the church is a beautiful and valuable asset, a 'green lung' for a town whose development has almost exclusively swept northwards.

◆

THE PARISH CHURCH 1891
The parish church started life as a small Norman church: there are small Norman windows and doorways at the north-west end of the nave. But it was largely rebuilt when it passed into the hands of nearby Rusper Priory, a Benedictine nunnery, in 1231. It then assumed its present scale, but it has been heavily restored and altered: for example, the row of gables along the aisle seen here date from 1865.

THE PARISH CHURCH 1891 29712

THE LOWER CAUSEWAY AND ST MARY'S CHURCH 1907 58191
The Causeway is a remarkable street leading south from the bustle of the town centre, a true 'backwater'. It was not always so, for it was South Street and the main route out of town to the south. Denne Park stopped all that, and the Worthing Road further west took over. Cut off from town by market infill, The Causeway is in a tranquil world on its own.

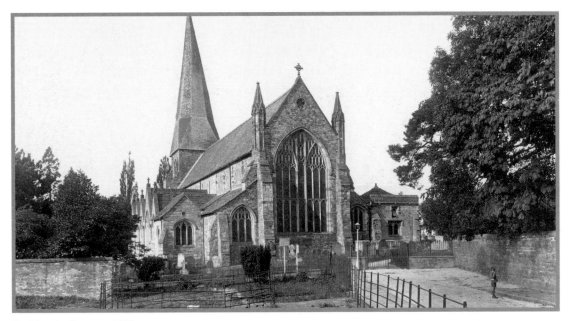

ST MARY'S CHURCH 1929 82449

From the east, in an area known as Normandy, the great east window dominates the view; it is an accurate copy, made in 1865, of the decayed original. To the left foreground now are the 1955 ranges added to St Mary's Almshouses, and on the right, behind the wall, is Normandy Gardens, modern Sussex tile-hung housing: the trees have gone.

OLD HOUSES 1927 79610A

Next to the churchyard is Flagstones, a house dated 1615 in the gable and roofed in Horsham stone slates, the flagstones of its name. Now a single dwelling, it has been much restored since the old motorcycles complete with acetylene lamps parked here. The railings have since been replaced by a stone wall.

THE CAUSEWAY 1898 41923
Looking south, this photograph gives a good view of the dense line of lime trees planted here in the 19th century. Due to disease they were all felled in 1940 and replanted, albeit in lesser numbers. The pavements, as in other parts of the town, are laid with huge slabs of Horsham stone, while Minstrels, the house on the right, has had its painted weatherboarding replaced by tile-hanging.

THE CAUSEWAY 1901 58194
In this view from the north end of The Causeway the lime avenue screens many of the buildings. To the right is now the national headquarters of the RSPCA in the 1704 Manor House, while to the left the Horsham Museum occupies No 9, the late 16th-century house with two leaning gables; it is timber-framed behind its render, and a fascinating local history museum.

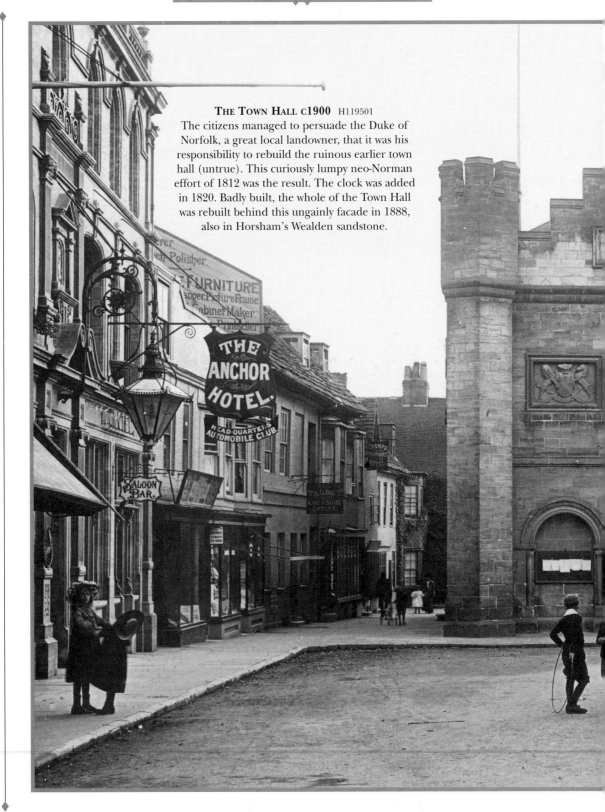

THE TOWN HALL c1900 H119501
The citizens managed to persuade the Duke of Norfolk, a great local landowner, that it was his responsibility to rebuild the ruinous earlier town hall (untrue). This curiously lumpy neo-Norman effort of 1812 was the result. The clock was added in 1820. Badly built, the whole of the Town Hall was rebuilt behind this ungainly facade in 1888, also in Horsham's Wealden sandstone.

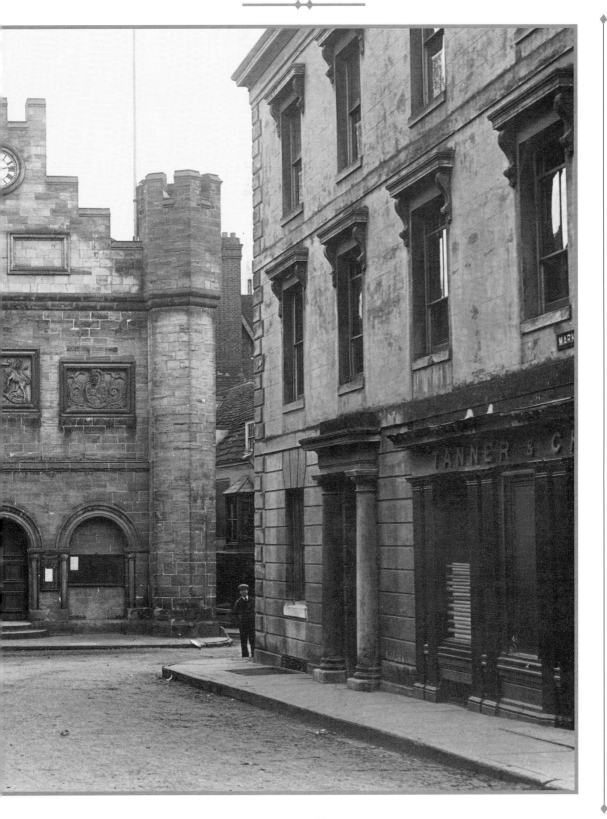

MARKET SQUARE c1955 H119067

The Duke, however, ensured that his coat of arms was one of the three in the panels above the Norman round arches of the entrance; the others were the Royal Arms and those of Horsham borough. One of the old Town Hall's principal virtues is that it separates the town centre's commercial bustle from The Causeway beyond, so perhaps one can forgive its ungainliness.

THE TOWN HALL 1923 73406
To the left of the Town Hall are two fine late 19th-century buildings. The one to the left, of 1894 has a longer facade along East Street, while the one beyond, dated 1899 and in an imposing Flemish style, was built as the Anchor Hotel. Here, it has become council offices, but nowadays it is a smart wine bar, Bar Vin.

THE TOWN HALL 1933 85573

In this view the photographer is looking south out of The Carfax into Market Place. The traffic policeman is controlling the traffic in East and West Streets which intersect here. To the left of the Town Hall's turrets is the narrow lane, now pedestrianised, leading into The Causeway. Ye Olde King's Head Hotel, apparently dating in part from 1401, still flourishes.

THE CARFAX C1960 H119117

The Carfax, the heart of Horsham's historic town, has been popular for years with painters, and more recently, of course, with photographers. The Frith Archive has many views of the Carfax, and this chapter contains enough to show its evolution from the 1890s to the 1960s.

LONDON ROAD (CARFAX WEST SIDE) 1891 29719

This is the earliest view in the book. It shows the west side, looking north into London Road. Everything on the left has been rebuilt since, and only the two far distant buildings survive of London Road. To give the reader his or her bearings, the house on the right is now the estate agents, King and Chasemore on the north side of The Carfax.

THE CARFAX 1907 58192
This view looks north. Past the bandstand in the centre of the
picture, Richmond Terrace on the left survives; but only the spire
of St Mark's was retained, to be surrounded by office blocks - of
which more later. The building of 1893 on the far right remains,
albeit a little simplified, and the 1897 Diamond Jubilee fountain
has been re-erected beyond the Albion Way inner ring road in
the shattered north end of inner North Street.

THE CARFAX 1898 41919

THE CARFAX 1898
The centrepiece of The Carfax central island is Frederick Wheeler's bank, now the Nat West. It is a proud building in plum brick, with rubbed red brick dressings and much Bath stone, and a plaque over the doorway informs us it was erected in 1897 'in the 60th year of the reign of Queen Victoria'. It now has a regrettable modern concrete-framed extension clad in strips of green slate and Bath stone.

◆

THE CARFAX 1924
When The Carfax was improved and partly pedestrianised in the early 1990s, the bandstand was relocated a few yards nearer the photographer. It was built by public subscription, a committee being formed in 1891. A Mr Sendall carried out the work, but the original subscription monies collected, £130, proved inadequate; a further £70 had to be raised before it opened amid great civic pomp in 1892.

THE CARFAX 1924 75332

THE CARFAX 1924 75329

There are only two Carfaxes in England, the other being in Oxford. It appears to be a word derived from the old French 'carrefourgs', or crossways, and is first recorded at Horsham in 1548, admittedly spelt differently as 'Scarfax'. Its location at the meeting of five roads is significant; of course, it is still the hub of the town.

THE CARFAX 1924 75333

This is the north side of The Carfax between London Road and North Street at the right. The fine bay-windowed house on the left is now a solicitor's office, while the town stocks in the railinged island in the foreground now rest, isolated, amid the York stone pavings of the recent pedestrianisation scheme.

THE CARFAX 1931 83413

The Carfax was once a very large triangular open market place, tapering from the wider north end southwards as far as The Causeway. The island of buildings on the right, which includes the Nat West Bank, is a later encroachment onto the market place when temporary market stalls and booths were replaced by permanent buildings.

THE CARFAX 1930 83411

By 1930 The Carfax has acquired a dignified War Memorial to the south of the bandstand, here hidden behind the fine tree. To the left are the stolid late Victorian rebuildings of much of the central island's east side's higgledy-piggledy market encroachments. Dignified by Dutch gables, they are a drabber contrast to the Queen Anne style of the Nat West bank beyond.

THE CARFAX 1933 85574

We are looking into Market Place, which is terminated by the odd neo-Norman Town Hall; to the left the long established newsagent, W S Parsons, has now been replaced by The Averys art gallery. At the right is the late 1920s Barclays Bank, a neo- Georgian building that was extended about 1960 to replace the rendered building, beyond the man up a ladder.

THE CARFAX 1933 85491

The east side of The Carfax retains some feel of its pre-Georgian character with this Horsham slab-roofed jettied Tudor timber-framed building, its timbers on this facade hidden by render. In the alley just out of view to the left leading to the modern Piries Place shopping centre you can see the timber-framing of its north flank elevation.

THE WAR MEMORIAL c1924 H119502
Erected on the east side of The Carfax, this memorial to Horsham's fallen in World War I had an inscription to the dead of World War II added subsequently. To the right is the taxi rank. The memorial is now relocated to the north side of The Carfax in the recent improvements. In this view the Armistice Day wreaths brighten up a fine November day.

THE CARFAX c1950 H119505
This view looks south along the west side of The Carfax. These buildings replaced those seen earlier in this chapter, on the left side of the 1891 view, number 29719. In the early 1950s the neo-Georgian shops and offices with three gabled projecting bays have just been completed and the offices newly let, while Peter Dominic's shop is still being fitted out.

THE CARFAX c1955 H119070
From the south-east this view looks beyond the bandstand and the motorcycles to the north side of The Carfax, with Richmond Terrace to the right. This was built as The Richmond Arms in the 18th century, and was altered in about 1840 into a terrace of houses with rather odd columned doorcases added. To the left is the old Post Office of the 1890s, now demolished.

THE CARFAX c1960 H119160

The north side of The Carfax is seen here before the demolition (to its undoubted detriment) of the central buildings; these were replaced by two office blocks, Grandford House and Ridgeland House. The pedimented building was the brewery offices of King and Barnes, the Horsham brewers, and the post office has now moved into its 1970s successor.

THE CARFAX c1960 H119102

This view looks north-east from beside The Crown Hotel, with its fine Doric fluted pilastered doorcase hidden by the lorry. This area is now transformed by the pedestrianisation of much of it, with traffic restricted to the east side and round the corner past the Crown. All this has made The Carfax a civilised place, and a far cry from the traffic-choked nightmare of the 1980s.

THE CARFAX c1960 H119124

Here we see the rebuilt north-west corner of the central island; the 1950s Pearl Assurance building is now occupied by a sandwich bar. Behind Richmond Terrace rears the roof of the old Odeon cinema in North Street, now replaced by Stane Court's tall office block. The third chapter takes us out of The Carfax into the surrounding streets of central Horsham.

WEST STREET c1955 H119044

This chapter heads west, then east and finally north from The Carfax on a brief tour of the town's main streets. Here we look along West Street from the South Street crossroads junction with West and Middle Streets. Chart and Lawrence, Horsham's long-established department store, now in 2000 closed and undergoing refurbishment, is on the right corner, and Lloyds TSB of the 1890s on the left corner.

WEST STREET c1960 H119159

Further east from photograph No 42851 shown on the next page, a 1950s Woolworth's represents the last gasp of Classical styles, while the buildings beyond were reconstructed as facades to the vast Swan Walk shopping centre in 1991. The Cafe in the distance on the corner of The Bishopric has gone; now rebuilt, it incorporates a McDonalds restaurant.

WEST STREET 1898 42851
There was much rebuilding in West Street from the
1890s on. Hunt Brothers' Italianate facade was
replaced after 1900 by a sub-Adamesque building,
seen on the left in photograph No H119044, with
delicate plaster festoons, bay windows and colonettes:
an architectural wedding cake of a facade. Note the
popular 1880s and 1890s crow-stepped Dutch revival
style in the brick buildings beyond.

WEST STREET c1960 H119123

THE BISHOPRIC c1960 H119187

WEST STREET c1960
Looking east, this is a much changed view: the left side was replaced by an office block and the modern Swan Walk shopping centre, and the Black Horse Hotel and the adjacent buildings beyond by a nasty 1960s development complete with coloured panels under the windows. The foreground is dominated by the modern Shelley Fountain, a remarkable 'cosmic cycle' sculpture with water by Angela Connor: an original and enjoyable water machine.

THE BISHOPRIC c1960
Again, all is changed in this view of The Bishopric, the westward continuation of West Street. The Green Dragon survives, a fine timber-framed early 17th-century building, but to its right all is rebuilt, and to its left the inner ring road, Albion Way, cuts its heartless dual carriageway through. The foreground has recently had a sculptural trail of boulders and a 'stream of life' installed.

THE BISHOPRIC c1960 H119131

THE BISHOPRIC c1960

Now cut off by Albion Way across the middle of this view, the malting oast, with its pyramidal slate roof topped by the cowl, marks the entrance to King and Barnes' Horsham brewery. The oast has since been demolished, and many of the other buildings along The Bishopric have been rebuilt, not usually for the better.

NORTH PARADE 1930

Heading north along Springfield Road, another battered fragment of the old town, you reach North Parade, which has Horsham Park on its right beyond the (still surviving) brick, then stone, wall on the right. To the left are the grounds of Springfield Park House, dating from the 1790s; these are now apartments in the centre of a new select housing estate, but many of the trees remain.

NORTH PARADE 1930 83416

LONDON ROAD c1960 H119114

We are back in the centre. This view of the south part of London Road has lost all but the two buildings in the far distance beyond Albion Way. The left side is occupied by the bulk of the Swan Walk shopping centre that now so dominates the centre of the town; even the old Capitol Theatre of 1923 was swept away - its forecourt is seen at the far left.

EAST STREET c1955 H119068

This view looks east along Middle Street, a narrow street linking West Street and East Street. The Olde King's Head is on the left, and the 1894 building on the right continues round into Market Place. The latter replaced Tudor jettied buildings. Middle Street was a main route through the town, and a tricky, narrow one for vehicles, until relatively recently.

EAST STREET 1891 29715

Here the photographer looks westwards from the Barttelot Road junction, with the narrow older part of East Street in the distance. The corner-towered building on the right, brand new in 1891, survives, now without the tower's pyramidal roof, as does the Dutch-style mission hall, dated 1891, beyond. The six gabled houses went for the Park Way dual carriageway, an eastward extension to Albion Way.

QUEEN STREET 1924 75334

Further east, beyond the railway bridge, East Street leads into Queen Street. The Alexandra Inn, an Arts and Crafts-style building of the early 20th century named after Edward VII's queen, is now Alexandra House. The late 19th-century stone shaped gables beyond have been rendered subsequently; opposite all has gone to make way for Nos 36-48 Queen Street, a modern two storey plus mansard office block.

BRIGHTON ROAD 1899 42853

Just beyond the view shown in photograph No 75334, Queen Street becomes Brighton Road. The chapel was demolished and rebuilt as Brighton Road Baptist Church in a fiery red Welsh brick soon after this view was taken. Beyond are some unusual mid 19th-century cottages, the outer ones bow-fronted, and further along Nos 17 to 27 of the 1880s survive, with their distinctive full height bay windows.

NORTH STREET 1924 75335

Back to Carfax, our tour heads north-west into North Street. The buildings on the right survive, as does the spire (and only the spire) of St Mark's Church, but all beyond the corner building on the left has gone. In any way you care to think of, North Street has suffered enormous indignities in the last twenty years, and has, in effect, ceased to exist.

NORTH STREET c1955 H119066

This is another sad view: the Odeon cinema with its bizarre 1930s lighthouse tower and all beyond has been swept away. This part of Horsham was sacrificed for the Albion Way inner relief road, and then for the office blocks of the Royal and Sun Alliance insurance company whose headquarters are in Horsham, while the Central Market's facade was rebuilt to front a recent Waitrose supermarket development.

NORTH STREET 1932 85028

No 26, the building with two bay windows on the left, survives, but all except the church spire has gone to make way for St Mark's Court, completed in 1991, which wraps around the retained tower and spire of St Mark's Church. On the right is Park Side, and beyond Albion Way is Stane Court, all offices for the Royal and Sun Alliance.

NORTH STREET c1955 H119065

St Mark's Church, rebuilt in 1870, was an uncompromising rock-faced effort, but it did not deserve its current indignity. The tower and spire of the church were retained, its lower stage becoming the Horsham Volunteers Bureau, and it is now within touching distance of the monumental and dwarfing St Mark's Court offices. A footbridge, Chart Way, over Albion Way rises to its west to complete the architectural humiliation of the remnant of the church.

NORTH STREET 1923 73402
In 1923 North Street beyond the town centre still had
fields on the east side. These are now occupied by office
blocks as development spread north towards the railway
station. St Mark's spire can be seen in the distance, while
on the right are the grounds of Horsham Park, although
Mr King's nurseryman and seedsman's business on the
right has gone and the buildings with it.

NORTH CHAPEL 1924 75332A

Nestling incongruously next to the tall 1953 telephone exchange to its right and not far from the station is North Chapel, a rambling timber-framed house of the 16th and 17th century with Horsham slab roofs. This old farmhouse was subdivided: the centre house is now the Northchapel Gallery. This view shows how rural this area was, even after the railway arrived in 1848.

NORTH STREET 1907 58193

Further along, on the opposite side of the road near its junction with Hurst Road, was this fine 15th-century hall and cross-wing farmhouse, here subdivided into four cottages. It has been replaced by modern housing that nods towards the original by having gables at each end. North Chapel was a hamlet of farmhouses and cottages that had the misfortune for the railway to build its station in its midst.

THE PARK, THE SWIMMING POOL 1934 86302

THE PARK
The Swimming Pool 1934
This chapter includes views of individually notable buildings and their grounds to the immediate north of the old town centre. They survived the town's expansion after the mid 19th century that mercifully washed around them, leaving them as green oases. This view shows the open-air swimming pool without which no town's park was considered complete in the 1930s.

HORSHAM PARK HOUSE 1929
This view shows the entrance front to Horsham Park House off North Street. Now offices for Horsham District Council, the front area is a car park and the building has been carefully repaired in recent years. The house was built in about 1720. This is the more ornate facade, in comparison with the garden front.

HORSHAM PARK HOUSE 1929 82446

THE PARK 1929 82447

THE PARK 1929

The garden front to Horsham Park is simpler, without the banded stone pilasters. It has a Horsham stone half-basement, but is mostly built in a mellow red brick with a Horsham stone slab roof. To its right is now a plum brick 1960s extension. The garden was entirely redesigned in 1991 by John Skelton, and includes a magnificent centrepiece sculptural sundial, named 'Sungod'.

THE PARK 1934

This view looks west, with Horsham Park House just out of view on the left. The outbuildings have been substantially reconstructed and have had a conservatory added to the end, and is now a cafeteria named The Conservatory. Skelton's garden is enclosed by his ornate fence and hedge screen, which now runs from the rockery parallel to the path.

THE PARK 1934 86303

THE SWIMMING POOL c1960 H119170

North-east of Horsham Park House is this open-air swimming pool, little changed since the 1934 view that opens this chapter. However, in the 1970s the pool was enclosed by a large building and is now an indoor pool, the Park Swimming Centre, so there need be no more shivering boys like the one seen on the other side of the pool.

THE HOSPITAL 1929 82445

Immediately north of Horsham Park, along Hurst Road, the town acquired a fine new hospital designed by the architect F C Troup and opened in July 1922. Built in a Lutyensesque Arts and Crafts style, it replaced the original Cottage hospital of 1892. This view is taken from the upper windows of Collyers School opposite.

THE HOSPITAL 1929 82443

This is now the Horsham Community Hospital. There has been much modern, mainly single-storey, expansion to the left of the original building, but it and its side wings remain remarkably unaltered. The main loss has been the hedged lawns and shrub beds, which have been replaced by car parking, although many of the original large cast concrete slabs survive.

THE GRAMMAR SCHOOL 1929 82442

Hurst Road was laid out in 1870, and in 1892 Collyer's Grammar School moved out here from the town centre. The school had been founded in 1532 by Richard Collyer, a Horsham lad who had been apprenticed at fifteen to a mercer (or merchant) in London, where he subsequently made his fortune; he used some of it to found a grammar school in his native town.

COLLYER'S SCHOOL C1930 H119503

The Victorian school was designed by Arthur Vernon, an architect from High Wycombe who designed large numbers of schools. Since this view was taken, the spirelet has gone, and large 1961 extensions have collided with the old building at the right. It is now a sixth-form college known as the College of Richard Collyer.

OLD COTTAGE GARDENS 1924 75339

One of the striking things about Horsham, and indeed many of the villages around it, is the odd mix of Victorian artisan housing with an intermingling of earlier houses of the 16th and 17th centuries. Typical Sussex Weald square panel timber-frames with yellow ochre washed infill panels below Horsham stone slate roofs peep out amid the later growth.

RUSPER ROAD C1960 H119154

Here, further north-east on the Rusper Road at Little Haven, is a good illustration of the somewhat characterless expansion of Horsham from the mid to late 19th century. There is late-Victorian housing on the left beyond a massive oak surviving from the old hedged country lane to Rusper, and more late-Victorian and 1950s housing on the right, typical of this expansionist phase.

CHRIST'S HOSPITAL 1907
Christ's Hospital School is an ancient foundation that in 1902 exchanged a hemmed-in site in Newgate Street, London, for the healthier climes of the Sussex Weald. The School had been founded in 1553 during the reign of Edward VI for poor children and orphans, and was based in the old buildings of the Greyfriars, a friary dissolved by Henry VIII in 1538.

CHRIST'S HOSPITAL
The Avenue 1907
The school is a vast complex, a small town even, and the spaciousness and scale of the buildings must have been a striking contrast to the old site in London for the transposed scholars. Here the photographer looks along The Avenue to the stone archway into the vast 'quad' at the centre of the school.

CHRIST'S HOSPITAL 1907 58196

CHRIST'S HOSPITAL, THE AVENUE 1907 58197

CHRIST HOSPITAL
Entrance to Quad and Dining Hall 1902 48692

The school was designed by Sir Aston Webb and Ingress Bell. The foundation stone was laid amid great ceremony on 23 October 1897, actually on Founder's Day, although work had started in 1893. These views are all taken in 1902, the year of its completion. The stone gateway of 1829 with its shaped gable and flanking pinnacles is perhaps the most ornate building in the school, and was brought from the London site.

CHRIST'S HOSPITAL, THE QUAD 1902 48690

This view gives some idea of the scale of the school. Its vast quad is as big as any barracks parade ground. The architecture dwarfs the pupils, and was probably made more austerely monumental by the Charity Commissioners: before they approved the designs, they trimmed out much ornament and artistic finish from the architects' designs on grounds of cost.

CHRIST'S HOSPITAL SCHOOL 1907 58198

All is on a stupendous scale: this is Aston Webb's Dining Hall, which is over one hundred and fifty feet long, and so high as to dwarf the pupils beneath its soaring ceilings. Inside is a huge painting by Verrio which occupies the bulk of one wall. All is in a mid-Tudor style, a homage presumably to the date of the school's original foundation.

CHRIST'S HOSPITAL, BIG SCHOOL 1902 48698

Big School, at the south end of the quad, is similarly vast; it is in fact the school hall. On its facade are two niches salvaged from the London school buildings containing the statues of Charles II and Sir John Moore. Again, the style is Tudor to Elizabethan, but less rich than originally intended: perhaps none the worse for that.

CHRIST'S HOSPITAL CHAPEL 1902 48695

The chapel is similarly monumental and overwhelming; its interior is distinguished by frescoes by Frank Brangwyn. The school, now a leading public school and co- educational since 1985, is noted for the boy's uniform of a belted dark blue coat, white neck bands and yellow socks, still worn during the day.

BARNS GREEN, THE VILLAGE c1960 B504027

Our tour of the environs of Horsham moves from the monumental grandeur of a public school to a much humbler scale at Barns Green, a couple of miles south-west of Christ's Hospital School. Here the photographer looks south-west past the village shop, which is located in one of a pair of cottages built in 1908. The shop has now gone, and a copy of the adjoining bay window replaces its shop window.

BARNS GREEN, HIGH STREET c1955 B504004

There are older buildings in Barns Green, but they are not visible in this view; for instance, set back between the pairs fronting the road is a timber-framed 16th-century house, Shyngells. To the left of the oaks is the green, now principally a sports fields with the pavilion and the Barns Green Village Club buildings on its south side.

BARNS GREEN, THE VILLAGE c1960 B504023

From near the point of photograph No B504004, the photographer rotated his camera to look east along Two Mile Ash Road, again with a number of semi-detached Edwardian cottages, some dated 1908, some 1910. The earlier house at the left, Cornerways, is earlier; beyond are six flats, Parkers, built after this view had been taken, replacing the ramshackle sheds.

ITCHINGFIELD, THE CHURCH c1960 173010

North of Barns Green is the picturesque church of St Nicholas with its shingled tower and spire, which is carried on enormous timbers visible inside the church. Of unique interest, however, is the Priest House, partly seen on the left. A 15th-century lodging for priests from Sele Priory who owned the church, it was extended in about 1600 to form almshouses: in either use it must have been amazingly cramped.

BROADBRIDGE HEATH
Portsmouth and Guildford Roads 1924 75469
It is surprising how informal roads still were in the
1920s: now there are pavements, kerbs, and road signs
here, and, on the Portsmouth Road, now the A264, a
very necessary pedestrian crossing. The Victorian pairs
of cottages remain; on the Guildford Road the old
school beyond the shops, opened in 1893, is now
houses, and the traffic has considerably increased.

BROADBRIDGE HEATH, GREENFIELD PLACE (SHELLEY'S BIRTHPLACE) 1923 74922

BROADBRIDGE HEATH
Greenfield Place (Shelley's Birthplace) 1923

The poet Percy Bysshe Shelley was born in 1792 in this attractive country house, which was built around 1678. Sent down from Oxford University and eloping, Shelley fell out with his father, Sir Bysshe, and was subsequently refused entry, but his boyhood was spent here. The house has Horsham stone roofs, and the sash windows are 18th-century, while the colonnaded loggia is 19th-century.

SLINFOLD
The Village Hall c1955

Slinfold is a very pretty village in rolling Weald country on a slope above the River Arun. The name means in Old English 'fold' (enclosure for animals) on a slope, and the village grew up just east of the old Roman road from London to Chichester. Fold, a common ending for Sussex villages, reflects Anglo-Saxon origins in which villages and estates had their stock grazing many miles north of their villages.

SLINFOLD, THE VILLAGE HALL c1955 S591001

SLINFOLD, THE POST OFFICE c1955 S591038

This delightful view in the centre of the village shows the characteristic chequer brick patterns popular in 18th- and 19th-century Sussex with grey double baked bricks alternating with reds. Slinfold House to the left has a Doric porch similar to others in the village; the shop is now a house, and the post office has migrated into the outbuilding to the right.

WARNHAM, THE COURT 1924 75345

North-east of Slinfold and north of Broadbridge Heath lies Warnham, four miles north-west of Horsham. Immediately south of the village is Warnham Court, now a school. Built in 1828 in an Elizabethan style, it had major additions by Blomfield in 1866, and further ones added by the school since this view was taken.

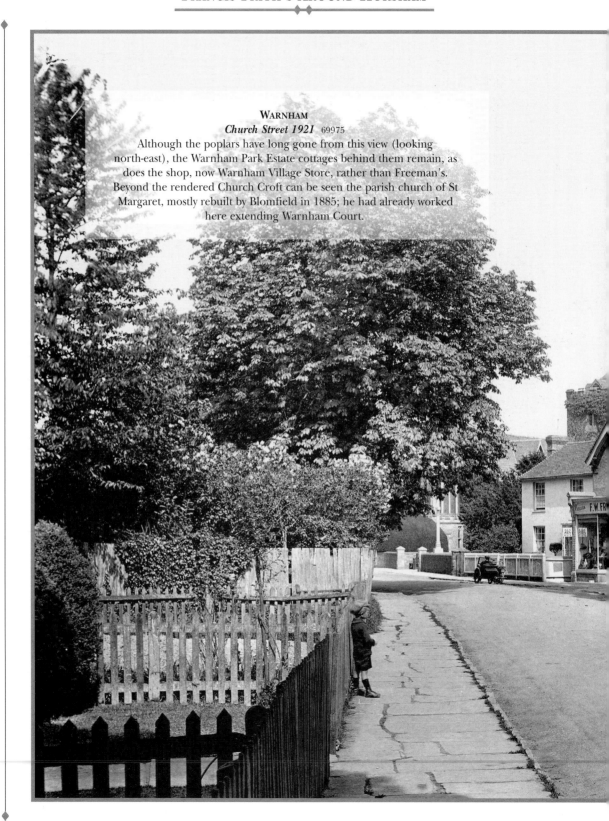

WARNHAM
Church Street 1921 69975
Although the poplars have long gone from this view (looking north-east), the Warnham Park Estate cottages behind them remain, as does the shop, now Warnham Village Store, rather than Freeman's. Beyond the rendered Church Croft can be seen the parish church of St Margaret, mostly rebuilt by Blomfield in 1885; he had already worked here extending Warnham Court.

WARNHAM, THE VILLAGE 1924 75353

This view looking south-west along Church Street has undergone much change: the building on the right has been replaced by recent housing, Hollands Way, and the farm buildings on the left have gone. However the Horsham stone-roofed Old Cottage and Stone Leigh and the houses next to them remain.

WARNHAM, FRIDAY STREET 1921 69974

Friday Street runs west from the south end of Church Street, and has an interesting range of cottages, from the mid 18th-century pair on the right in brick with a Horsham slate hipped roof to Victorian pairs of cottages. The weatherboarded ones beyond have been demolished for St Margaret's Court, a group of small houses.

WARNHAM, THE VILLAGE 1927 79579

This view looks south down School Hill towards the churchyard beyond the junction with Bell Road. The cottages are virtually unchanged, with Peppercorn Cottage on the left and the two gables and jetty of 16th-century Shatherum beyond. The village forge and wheelwright's shop is behind the array of wheels in the distance; the forge now a house called, unsurprisingly, The Old Forge.

WARNHAM, CORNER HOUSE 1921 69980

East of the village at the end of Bell Street is the Dorking road, now the busy A24. Although the junction has been much 'improved', Cowslip Cottage and No 57 remain; the walls on the right are to the grounds of Westons Place. The open-topped bus from Horsham has just collected passengers from Warnham and is setting off for Redhill via Dorking.

FAYGATE, THE VILLAGE 1929 82454

Faygate is little more than a hamlet that expanded after the railway came to Horsham; it was a branch from the London Brighton and South Coast Railway via Three Bridges near Crawley. Faygate still has a station, but it remains a rural settlement with mainly later 19th-century pairs of cottages, some here dated 1881.

HOLMBUSH TOWER 1927 79621
This tall 19th-century stone folly tower, built for the owners of the 1820s Gothicky Holmbush house, gave wide views over Holmbush Forest and St Leonard's Forest; it was never as well-known as the less secluded Leith Hill Tower over the border in Surrey.

ST LEONARD'S FOREST 1927 79618
St Leonard's Forest is the westernmost of the great Sussex forests that were planted on the thin, barren soils of the High Weald. Ashdown Forest, south of East Grinstead, is the best known and most accessible. St Leonard's, named after a former chapel, was re-planted after tile drains were laid in the 1840s, for previous 18th-century attempts in this barren, ill drained soil had foundered.

Index

Bishopric 48, 49

Brighton Road 52-53

Carfax 33, 34-35, 36, 37, 38, 39, 41, 42-43, 44

Causeway 21, 25, 27

Collyer's School 63

Cricket Ground 20

East Street 50, 51

Flagstones 26

Garden of Remembrance 23

General View 18-19, 20

Grammar School 62

Horsham Park 59, 60

Hospital 61, 62

London Road 33, 50

Market Square 30

Mill Bay 22, 24

North Chapel 37, 58

North Parade 49, 52-53

North Street 54, 55, 56-57, 58

Queen Street 51

River Arun 22

Rusper Road 64

St Mary's Church 21, 24, 25, 26

Swimming Pool 59, 61

Town Hall 28-29, 31, 32, 33

Town Mill 23

War Memorial 40

West Street 45, 46-47, 48

AROUND HORSHAM

Barns Green 70, 71

Broadbridge Heath 72-73, 74

Christ's Hospital School 65, 66-67, 68, 69

Faygate 80

Holmbush Tower 81

Itchingfield 71

Slinfold 74, 75

St Leonard's Forest 82

Warnham 75, 76-77, 78, 79

Frith Book Co Titles

Frith Book Company publish over a 100 new titles each year. For latest catalogue please contact Frith Book Co.

Town Books 96pp, 100 photos. County and Themed Books 128pp, 150 photos
(unless specified) All titles hardback laminated case and jacket
except those indicated pb (paperback)

Around Barnstaple	1-85937-084-5	£12.99
Around Blackpool	1-85937-049-7	£12.99
Around Bognor Regis	1-85937-055-1	£12.99
Around Bristol	1-85937-050-0	£12.99
Around Cambridge	1-85937-092-6	£12.99
Cheshire	1-85937-045-4	£14.99
Around Chester	1-85937-090-X	£12.99
Around Chesterfield	1-85937-071-3	£12.99
Around Chichester	1-85937-089-6	£12.99
Cornwall	1-85937-054-3	£14.99
Cotswolds	1-85937-099-3	£14.99
Around Derby	1-85937-046-2	£12.99
Devon	1-85937-052-7	£14.99
Dorset	1-85937-075-6	£14.99
Dorset Coast	1-85937-062-4	£14.99
Around Dublin	1-85937-058-6	£12.99
East Anglia	1-85937-059-4	£14.99
Around Eastbourne	1-85937-061-6	£12.99
English Castles	1-85937-078-0	£14.99
Around Falmouth	1-85937-066-7	£12.99
Hampshire	1-85937-064-0	£14.99
Isle of Man	1-85937-065-9	£14.99
Around Maidstone	1-85937-056-X	£12.99
North Yorkshire	1-85937-048-9	£14.99
Around Nottingham	1-85937-060-8	£12.99
Around Penzance	1-85937-069-1	£12.99
Around Reading	1-85937-087-X	£12.99
Around St Ives	1-85937-068-3	£12.99
Around Salisbury	1-85937-091-8	£12.99
Around Scarborough	1-85937-104-3	£12.99
Scottish Castles	1-85937-077-2	£14.99
Around Sevenoaks and Tonbridge	1-85937-057-8	£12.99

Sheffield and S Yorkshire	1-85937-070-5	£14.99
Shropshire	1-85937-083-7	£14.99
Staffordshire	1-85937-047-0 (96pp)	£12.99
Suffolk	1-85937-074-8	£14.99
Surrey	1-85937-081-0	£14.99
Around Torbay	1-85937-063-2	£12.99
Wiltshire	1-85937-053-5	£14.99
Around Bakewell	1-85937-113-2	£12.99
Around Bournemouth	1-85937-067-5	£12.99
Cambridgeshire	1-85937-086-1	£14.99
Essex	1-85937-082-9	£14.99
Around Great Yarmouth	1-85937-085-3	£12.99
Hertfordshire	1-85937-079-9	£14.99
Isle of Wight	1-85937-114-0	£14.99
Around Lincoln	1-85937-111-6	£12.99
Oxfordshire	1-85937-076-4	£14.99
Around Shrewsbury	1-85937-110-8	£12.99
South Devon Coast	1-85937-107-8	£14.99
Around Stratford upon Avon	1-85937-098-5	£12.99
West Midlands	1-85937-109-4	£14.99

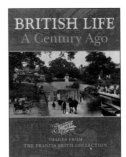

British Life A Century Ago
246 x 189mm
144pp, hardback.
Black and white
Lavishly illustrated with photos
from the turn of the century,
and with extensive commentary.
It offers a unique insight into
the social history and heritage
of bygone Britain.

1-85937-103-5 £17.99

Available from your local bookshop or from the publisher

Frith Book Co Titles Available in 2000

Around Bath	1-85937-097-7	£12.99	Mar
County Durham	1-85937-123-x	£14.99	Mar
Cumbria	1-85937-101-9	£14.99	Mar
Down the Thames	1-85937-121-3	£14.99	Mar
Around Exeter	1-85937-126-4	£12.99	Mar
Greater Manchester	1-85937-108-6	£14.99	Mar
Around Guildford	1-85937-117-5	£12.99	Mar
Around Harrogate	1-85937-112-4	£12.99	Mar
Around Leicester	1-85937-073-x	£12.99	Mar
Around Liverpool	1-85937-051-9	£12.99	Mar
Around Newark	1-85937-105-1	£12.99	Mar
Northumberland and Tyne & Wear			
	1-85937-072-1	£14.99	Mar
Around Oxford	1-85937-096-9	£12.99	Mar
Around Plymouth	1-85937-119-1	£12.99	Mar
Around Southport	1-85937-106-x	£12.99	Mar
Welsh Castles	1-85937-120-5	£14.99	Mar
Around Belfast	1-85937-094-2	£12.99	Apr
Canals and Waterways	1-85937-129-9	£17.99	Apr
Down the Severn	1-85937-118-3	£14.99	Apr
East Sussex	1-85937-130-2	£14.99	Apr
Exmoor	1-85937-132-9	£14.99	Apr
Gloucestershire	1-85937-102-7	£14.99	Apr
Around Horsham	1-85937-127-2	£12.99	Apr
Around Ipswich	1-85937-133-7	£12.99	Apr
Ireland (pb)	1-85937-181-7	£9.99	Apr
Kent Living Memories	1-85937-125-6	£14.99	Apr
London (pb)	1-85937-183-3	£9.99	Apr
New Forest	1-85937-128-0	£14.99	Apr
Scotland (pb)	1-85937-182-5	£9.99	Apr
Around Southampton	1-85937-088-8	£12.99	Apr
Stone Circles & Ancient Monuments			
	1-85937-143-4	£17.99	Apr
Sussex (pb)	1-85937-184-1	£9.99	Apr
Colchester (pb)	1-85937-188-4	£8.99	May
County Maps of Britain			
	1-85937-156-6 (192pp)	£19.99	May
Leicestershire (pb)	1-85937-185-x	£9.99	May

Lincolnshire	1-85937-135-3	£14.99	May
Around Newquay	1-85937-140-x	£12.99	May
Nottinghamshire (pb)	1-85937-187-6	£9.99	May
Redhill to Reigate	1-85937-137-x	£12.99	May
Victorian & Edwardian Yorkshire			
	1-85937-154-x	£14.99	May
Around Winchester	1-85937-139-6	£12.99	May
Yorkshire (pb)	1-85937-186-8	£9.99	May
Berkshire (pb)	1-85937-191-4	£9.99	Jun
Brighton (pb)	1-85937-192-2	£8.99	Jun
Dartmoor	1-85937-145-0	£14.99	Jun
East London	1-85937-080-2	£14.99	Jun
Glasgow (pb)	1-85937-190-6	£8.99	Jun
Kent (pb)	1-85937-189-2	£9.99	Jun
Victorian & Edwardian Kent			
	1-85937-149-3	£14.99	Jun
North Devon Coast	1-85937-146-9	£14.99	Jun
Peak District	1-85937-100-0	£14.99	Jun
Around Truro	1-85937-147-7	£12.99	Jun
Victorian & Edwardian Maritime Album			
	1-85937-144-2	£17.99	Jun
West Sussex	1-85937-148-5	£14.99	Jun
Churches of Berkshire	1-85937-170-1	£17.99	Jul
Churches of Dorset	1-85937-172-8	£17.99	Jul
Churches of Hampshire	1-85937-207-4	£17.99	Jul
Churches of Wiltshire	1-85937-171-x	£17.99	Jul
Derbyshire (pb)	1-85937-196-5	£9.99	Jul
Edinburgh (pb)	1-85937-193-0	£8.99	Jul
Herefordshire	1-85937-174-4	£14.99	Jul
Norwich (pb)	1-85937-194-9	£8.99	Jul
Ports and Harbours	1-85937-208-2	£17.99	Jul
Somerset and Avon	1-85937-153-1	£14.99	Jul
South Devon Living Memories			
	1-85937-168-x	£14.99	Jul
Warwickshire (pb)	1-85937-203-1	£9.99	Jul
Worcestershire	1-85937-152-3	£14.99	Jul
Yorkshire Living Memories			
	1-85937-166-3	£14.99	Jul

FRITH PRODUCTS & SERVICES

Francis Frith would doubtless be pleased to know that the pioneering publishing venture he started in 1860 still continues today. More than a hundred and thirty years later, The Francis Frith Collection continues in the same innovative tradition and is now one of the foremost publishers of vintage photographs in the world. Some of the current activities include:

Interior Decoration

Today Frith's photographs can be seen framed and as giant wall murals in thousands of pubs, restaurants, hotels, banks, retail stores and other public buildings throughout the country. In every case they enhance the unique local atmosphere of the places they depict and provide reminders of gentler days in an increasingly busy and frenetic world.

Product Promotions

Frith products have been used by many major companies to promote the sales of their own products or to reinforce their own history and heritage. Brands include Hovis bread, Courage beers, Scots Porage Oats, Colman's mustard, Cadbury's foods, Mellow Birds coffee, Dunhill pipe tobacco, Guinness, and Bulmer's Cider.

Genealogy and Family History

As the interest in family history and roots grows world-wide, more and more people are turning to Frith's photographs of Great Britain for images of the towns, villages and streets where their ancestors lived; and, of course, photographs of the churches and chapels where their ancestors were christened, married and buried are an essential part of every genealogy tree and family album.

A series of easy-to-use CD Roms is planned for publication, and an increasing number of Frith photographs will be able to be viewed on specialist genealogy sites. A growing range of Frith books will be available on CD.

The Internet

Already thousands of Frith photographs can be viewed and purchased on the internet. By the end of the year 2000 some 60,000 Frith photographs will be available on the internet. The number of sites is constantly expanding, each focussing on different products and services from the Collection.
Some of the sites are listed below.

www.townpages.co.uk
www.icollector.com
www.barclaysquare.co.uk
www.cornwall-online.co.uk

For background information on the Collection look at the three following sites:

www.francisfrith.com
www.francisfrith.co.uk
www.frithbook.co.uk

Frith Products

All Frith photographs are available Framed or just as Mounted Prints, and can be ordered from the address below. From time to time other products - Address Books, Calendars, Table Mats, etc - are available.

For further information:
if you would like further information on any of the above aspects of the Frith business please contact us at the address below:
The Francis Frith Collection,
Frith's Barn, Teffont, Salisbury, Wiltshire,
England SP3 5QP.
Tel: +44 (0)1722 716 376 Fax: +44 (0)1722 716 881   Email: uksales@francisfrith.com

To receive your FREE Mounted Print

Cut out this Voucher and return it with your remittance for £1.50 to cover postage and handling. Choose any photograph included in this book. Your SEPIA print will be A4 in size, and mounted in a cream mount with burgundy rule lines, overall size 14 x 11 inches.

Order additional Mounted Prints at HALF PRICE (only £7.49 each*)

If there are further pictures you would like to order, possibly as gifts for friends and family, acquire them at half price (no additional postage and handling required).

Have your Mounted Prints framed*

For an additional £14.95 per print you can have your chosen Mounted Print framed in an elegant polished wood and gilt moulding, overall size 16 x 13 inches (no additional postage and handling required).

---

* IMPORTANT!
These special prices are only available if ordered using the original voucher on this page (no copies permitted) and at the same time as your free Mounted Print, for delivery to the same address

---

Frith Collectors' Guild

From time to time we publish a magazine of news and stories about Frith photographs and further special offers of Frith products. If you would like 12 months FREE membership, please return this form.

Send completed forms to:
The Francis Frith Collection, Frith's Barn, Teffont, Salisbury, Wiltshire SP3 5QP

Voucher for FREE and Reduced Price Frith Prints

Picture no.	Page number	Qty	Mounted @ £7.49	Framed + £14.95	Total Cost
		1	**Free of charge***	£	£
			£7.49	£	£
			£7.49	£	£
			£7.49	£	£
			£7.49	£	£
			£7.49	£	£
			* Post & handling		£1.50
Book Title			**Total Order Cost**		**£**

Please do not photocopy this voucher. Only the original is valid, so please cut it out and return it to us.

I enclose a cheque / postal order for £ . . . . made payable to 'The Francis Frith Collection' OR please debit my Mastercard / Visa / Switch / Amex card

Number . . . .

Expires . . . . Signature . . . .

Name Mr/Mrs/Ms . . . .

Address . . . .

. . . .

. . . .

. . . . Postcode . . . .

Daytime Tel No . . . .   Valid to 31/12/01

The Francis Frith Collectors' Guild

Please enrol me as a member for 12 months free of charge.

Name Mr/Mrs/Ms . . . .

Address . . . .

. . . .

. . . .

. . . . Postcode . . . .

Free Print - see overleaf